Pretty Pieces

D1808240

Charles Robertson

Published by

Bottle Tree Productions

CONTENTS

Acknowledgments

Actors Leigh Ann Bellamy and Zorba Dravillas helped shape the original play. Their input was an essential part of the creative process. For a writer/director to have actors to bounce ideas off is naturally of tremendous benefit.

Notes about the Play

Pretty Pieces is a one act play about a brother and sister who are trapped in a toxic relationship. They were likely abused as kids. I say likely, because the characters don't tell us. It has been blotted from the girl's memory and the boy remembers, but he doesn't want to talk about it. Many people who are abused or suffer some sort of Post Traumatic Stress don't want to remember the trauma. They are often in denial. I thought it would be unrealistic to explain why they are the way they are, too simplistic. While doctors have a checklist of diagnoses and cures, writers don't. Part of the reason for not providing a way out, an answer, is to trap the audience in these two doomed people's lives, to make the audience feel what they feel. Most people in real life don't know why they are the way they are, why they do the things that they do. The Girl is trying to fit the pieces of their lives together, to figure out what happened to them, to figure out why they are the way that they are. She finds some old pictures and an old report card but these clues are not enough for her to figure out the true horror of their past. And the Boy won't tell. The Boy tries to forget but can't. The Boy copes by using drugs and selling his body. The Girl copes by building her own psychological and emotional cage, trapping her in the apartment. She can't escape her personal prison, because she is afraid of the outside world. To add fuel to the emotional fire, they are being evicted. The Boy thinks he has found a way out. An older man has invited the Boy to come and live with him. The Girl falls apart when she hears this. She is going to make sure that neither of them will ever leave.

v

Charles Robertson

Act One

The setting is a run-down apartment. It does not need to be realistic. It is a personal hell. There should be an old couch, a small table and two chairs, a dresser a mattress on the floor and a small baby crib. There can be other furniture, but those are the basics. When the lights go down there is the sound of a young woman singing a song that one would sing to a baby- such as 'Hush little baby"

When the lights come up, it is a Red light only. The red light symbolizes darkness. It is also a not-so- subtle reference to hell, as in the characters are living in their own personal hell.

1

Pretty Pieces

A young woman enters carrying a baby. She is wearing a dress. It should not be in great shape. She sings softly to it as she sets the table with mismatched cutlery and plates. She then sits down and starts to look through photographs.

GIRL: *(Holding a doll in her arms. Pictures spread out on the floor before her. Tentatively she puts one picture beside another, considers it, and then moves it beside another, as if she is putting together some sort of jigsaw puzzle-She becomes stressed and starts getting more and more aggressive as she tries to make the pictures fit together somehow-She stops)*

See. That's me there on the pony. You ever ride a pony? And that's my brother. See, he's cryin'. He's scared of the pony. He's a scaredy cat. And that's him on his bike, and me. See this one there. That must be me at my birthday party, blowin' out the candles on my cake. Eight candles. See. Eight years old. And look at this. Look at this. Did you see my report card? Wanna know what it says here? It says that I have potential. That's what my report card says. I have potential. I used to be real smart when I was little. See…and I could write good…I just…I just….I just don't know where everythin' goes. How it works. Like I know that everythin' has to fit. I know it all has

2

to mean sumthin'. And there's this. Look. I acted in a play. I'm an actor. See, it says that here. Why? Why did I do that? My brother; he says that everythin' means sumthin'. There's a reason for stuff. There's a reason why it's there. *(A young man enters with a backpack. He sees the room is dark and turns on the light switch and the stage brightens-The red goes out-He goes to a dresser, and rifles through it for clothes. He can be in a dark t-shirt-preferrably black and jeans)*

GIRL: What are you doin?

BOY: Leavin'.

GIRL: Wait! Look what I found. These pictures of when we were little, I found them under the couch. I was lookin' for Baby's shoes and I found these pictures. What are you doin'?

BOY: *(Taking clothes out of the dresser)* I'm leavin'. I'm out of here.

GIRL: What are you talkin' about?

BOY: I'm goin'.

GIRL: Why are you takin' your clothes?

BOY: 'Cause, like I said, I'm goin'. I'm leavin', so I need my clothes.

GIRL: *(Gets up)* You don't need your clothes! Why do you need your clothes?

BOY: Like I said, I'm leavin'. I'm leavin' for good. I'm movin' out!

GIRL: *(Moves toward him)* You can't leave.

BOY: Yeah, I can. I'm doin' it, aren't I?

GIRL: I won't let you. *(Putting clothes back in the dresser)*

BOY: *(Pleading)* Please, just don't make this any harder than it is.

GIRL: I'm puttin' them back. These clothes gotta go back. You're gonna get 'em all messy. I clean up. I put things away all nice and tidy and you take 'em out and throw 'em all over the place.

BOY: No. *(Fighting for the clothes)* I'm leavin'. I gotta be somewhere. Somebody's waitin'. Somebody's waitin' for me, and I gotta go. I made a promise.

GIRL: I told you. Put 'em back. *(Grabbing the clothes from the knapsack)*

BOY: And who do you think you are? The Queen of freakin' England?

GIRL: *(Folding the clothes roughly)* At least I have potential. That's more n' some people. My teacher, my grade three teacher said that, Mrs. Kripshaw. Remember her? Mrs. Kripshaw. She said I had potential, said that I wrote neatly. Remember the birthday party. *(Forgets about the clothes)* After the birthday party, everythin' stopped. Everythin' just stopped, I dunno. Everythin' just stopped and waited, I don't know for what…It was like the world ended. But a long time ago, somebody thought I was special.

BOY: *(Contemptuous)* Special? You think you're special? You think you're so great? Well, you're not, you're nuthin'. Under our clothes we're all the same. We're just flesh and bone. We rot and stink.

GIRL: *(Not wanting to hear negative thoughts)* Not me. I told you. I'm special.

BOY: *(Sarcastically)* You're special all right.

GIRL: So are you.

BOY: So am I what?

GIRL: Special…like me. You and me, we're special. And Baby, too. *(Hugs the baby close and then speaks baby-talk to the baby)* Yes you are.

BOY: *(Without emotion)* I'm not special. I've been out there, out there in the world, and you should see what I've seen. *(Sits down on the wretched couch)* There are a hundred people like me, a thousand, a million special people like me. No money, no hope, no dreams. Shadow people. Background people. People that live in the dark, in alleyways, on sidewalks, in ditches, people that live in rundown apartments like this rundown apartment.

GIRL: *(She becomes almost child-like)* Did you forget?

BOY: *(Irritated)* What? What did I forget? What did I forget this time?

GIRL: Did you forget what day it is?

BOY: *(Distracted)* I dunno. Tuesday, isn't it?

GIRL: Nope.

BOY: No? It's not Tuesday?

GIRL: No, It might be Tuesday, (*As if she has some big secret*) but it also might be another day.

BOY: *(Exasperated)* Another day? Wednesday?

GIRL: No silly, it might be my birthday.

BOY: It might be your birthday? Don't you know? Don't you friggin' know if it's your birthday or not?

GIRL: *(Suddenly a woman)* No, I mean, I know it's my birthday. I know it. Why do you tease me? You can't go today. You always tease me. You always say you're leavin'. *(Back to being child-like)* Did you bring me sumthin'? Did you bring me sumthin' special?

BOY: No.

GIRL: *(Pressing)* Yes you did.

BOY: No, I didn't.

GIRL: *(Like an excited little girl)* You're hidin' sumthin'. I can tell.

BOY: No, I'm not.

GIRL: Yes you are.

BOY: *(Emotionless)* No, I'm not hidin' nuthin'. I don't have nuthin'. I can't afford nuthin'.

GIRL: *(Whiny)* Why not? Why didn't you remember?

BOY: I dunno. *(Goes back to packing his bag)* I just forgot. You didn't remind me.

GIRL: Why do I have to remind you? Why should I have to remind you? You should know. You should have remembered.

BOY: How am I sposed to remember every little thing?

GIRL: It's not some little thing. It's big. Birthdays are big. Birthdays are like a big clock, a big clock that tells a story. Only the story isn't about someone else. It's about you, your own special story. And people that are close to you, they should remember your story. That story should be special to them, too. You should know that. I remembered your birthday. On your birthday, I made you sumthin'. I made you sumthin' special.

BOY: *(Goes over to the table and picks up some deformed knick-knack)* Yeah, you made this.

GIRL: Didn't you like it?

BOY: *(Appraising it)* I dunno. It's stupid. I don't know what it is.

GIRL: *(Angry)* It's not stupid. *(Softer)* It's the thought that counts. That's what they say isn't it? That it's the thought that counts? So what about me? All I wanted was a cake, a cake with vanilla icin'. That's all I wanted. A nice cake with vanilla icin' and candles. Why couldn't you get me a cake like that? *(Like a three year old)* I like cake.

BOY: *(Trying to be rational and patient)* But I couldn't…I couldn't buy you nuthin'. I'm busted. I didn't have no money.

GIRL: *(As if she is his wife)* You never have money. I'm the one. I'm the one that puts food on the table.

BOY: *(Angry)* Only I have to go and get it. I mean you don't go out and get it, do you. You don't go out. You don't go out for anythin', anytime. The cheque comes to the door, and I have to go out like Joe Shmo, I'm sick of it! I have to stand in line like one of them losers at the Supermarket. You know the ones I mean, the ones that play the game, that live in that dream,

GIRL: I know. You're different. *(To the baby)* He's special. He's a bum!

BOY: Don't call me that.

GIRL: *(To the baby again)* He's a loser!

BOY: *(Smoldering)* I'm warnin' you.

GIRL: *(Daring him to hit her)* A drug addict! A prostitute! A pervert!

BOY: *(Angry)* Shut up!

GIRL: *(To the baby)* He's a dirty, disgustin', stupid, disgustin' drug addict!

BOY: *(Starts toward her)* Shut up!

GIRL: *(Backing away frightened)* Keep away from me! Stay away from me!

BOY: *(He stops)* Are you finished?

GIRL: I just don't know how you could forget. How could you forget? It only comes by once a year, my special day, my another year older day You like cake, don't you?...Cakes with candles on them. Did you get any? Did you get any cake?

BOY: I dunno. Like I said, I just didn't remember.

GIRL: *(Faraway look as if seeing a party in the distance)* Didn't remember? Didn't remember about the party?

BOY: *(Angry)* No, you know I didn't remember about no goddamn party!

GIRL: …and balloons. Couldn't you get no balloons?

BOY: *(Resigned)* No,

GIRL: *(Earnestly)* 'Cause for birthdays you need balloons, else how's anyone sposed to know that it's a party?

BOY: I didn't get no balloons.

GIRL: And cake with vanilla icin'. Did I tell you that? Did I tell you that before? And my name in letters. And flowers on it. I always save the flowers for last. I like cake.

BOY: *(Frustrated with her not listening)* I didn't get no freakin' cake! I didn't get nuthin'.

GIRL: *(Suddenly all grown up)* Today we got a notice.

BOY: What kind of notice?

GIRL: He's kickin' us out.

BOY: Who? Who's doin' that? Who's kickin' us out?

GIRL: The landlord. The landlord says we owe him four months rent… I thought you paid him. Didn't you pay him?

BOY: *(Evasively)* I dunno

GIRL: You take my cheques. You take my cheques and you're supposed to pay the rent with it. You take my cheques and the money is gone. *(Pushes him)* Where is the money, huh? *(Pushes him again)* Where is the money I gave you? Where is it? *(Pushes him a third time)* Huh? Where is my money? 'Cause I haven't ate nuthin', I don't know how long I ate last. *(Dreamily)* I keep thinkin' of the cake. I dream about it. The candles on it are glowing like little angels, like I'm in heaven, and I can taste the icin'. *(Growing agitated)* I ain't ever had no icin' since when I was eight. I'm so hungry. I'm gonna disappear without no food.

BOY: I didn't get nuthin' to eat. I didn't get you nuthin' to eat Nobody got nuthin' to eat, 'cause I don't got no money.

GIRL: But, you're out there in the world. There's food out there, garbage out there, You can eat garbage, but what is there here? Nuthin'. There's nuthin' here, nuthin' but me, *(Growing concern about the baby)* And the baby. What about the baby? How's the baby gonna survive? How's the baby gonna live?

BOY: Hate to break it to you but that fuckin' thing ain't real. What it is, is frightenin'. *(He picks up his bag)*

GIRL: *(Holding the baby close to her protectively)* Don't say that. Don't say that in front of the baby. What are you doin? *(Lays the baby in the crib and runs after him)*

BOY: *(Stops on his way to the door)* I told you, I'm going. I met someone.

GIRL: *(Sadly)* You met someone?

BOY: Yeah, I met someone.

GIRL: Who was it? Who did you meet?

BOY: *(With an air of finality)* Someone. Somebody. I'm gonna move in with them.

GIRL: Move in with them?

BOY: *(Frustrated with her, but anxious to get it all out in the open)* Him! I'm gonna move in with him. He has money.

GIRL: Money? Stupid' money? This is about stupid goddamn shit hole money!

BOY: *(Shrugs)* Well, money makes the world go round and like I said, I ain't had no money in so long. I just stopped in to say goodbye. Get my clothes.

GIRL: *(Pathetically)* But it's my birthday. You can't just- How am I gonna survive? How am I gonna survive without you?

BOY: *(Backing away)* Don't. Don't do this. Don't do this to me.

GIRL: *(Reaching out for him)* What? What am I doin'? What's the problem? What am I doin' to you? What did I ever do to you?

BOY: What you're doin'.

GIRL: And what am I doin'? I'm not doin' nuthin'.

BOY: *(Confronting her)* You're playin' games. You're tryin' to keep me here, tryin' to make me feel guilty, tryin' to make me feel that I owe you, that I owe you obligations, but see, its not like that. He says I don't owe you nuthin'.

GIRL: He says. Someone says, some guy says, and now you're out of here.

BOY: Yeah, that's it. Simon says and I'm outta here. *(Trying to break through her madness)* You gotta get outta here, too. It's crazy. This is crazy. This ain't real. You gotta fight. You're drownin', and you don't even know it.

GIRL: *(Touching him)* What are you sayin' to me? That you're just gonna abandon me. Just like that. Bye, bye. See you later. We're brother and sister, flesh and blood. We can't just break up, break apart. We're connected. We're blood.

BOY: *(Paralyzed-unable to move)* Don't make it so hard. Don't make it so hard on me.

GIRL: On you? On you?...It's not hard on you. How's it hard on you? What's so tough about bein' you? It's me. You know that. It's me. What can I do? How will I eat? I can't go out there. You know I can't go out there. Outside. Its gonna swallow me up. I'll die. I won't be able to breathe. I can't go out there.

Who's gonna pay the rent? Whose gonna take care of me?

BOY: *(Holding her gently)* Hush. Calm down. Maybe I can drop by. Like I said; my friend, he has money. I'm sure I can swing by and get you some food, some help.

GIRL: *(Pushes away from him)* Help? What are you talkin' about? What the hell are you talking about? I don't need help. Are you sayin' I need help? I don't need help. What are you talkin' bout? Like a doctor or sumthin'? You think I need some kind of help like that, you think I need a doctor or sumthin? You think I need that kind of help?

BOY: You know you need help.

GIRL: Why don't you just get the hell out of here. Why don't you just…fuck off and get the hell out of here!

BOY: *(His turn to be pathetic)* Don't be like that. Don't be so pitiful. Don't make me stay. It'll kill me. If I have to stay here, it'll fuckin' kill me.

GIRL: I'm not stoppin' you. Who's stoppin' you? If you really want to go, Go! I hate you anyway. You're one pathetic loser. You take all my money and stick it up your arm. Who needs you, who needs you, you little maggot! Stupid pathetic little boy. You never grew up, did you, you never learned how, You're just some stupid kid inside a man's body. That's right, ain't it? You're nuthin'!

BOY: *(Turns to go)* Fine. Bye.

GIRL: *(Without looking, picks up a spoon from the table)* Stop! If you leave I'll kill myself.

BOY: With that?

GIRL: *(Looks at spoon in her hand and then grabs a sharp knife)* This! I'll kill myself with this!

BOY: Put that down before you hurt someone.

GIRL: *(Jabbing the knife at him)* That's the point. I don't want to, but I'll do it if I have to. I'll kill myself if I have to.

BOY: No you won't! You're always talkin' like that, Talkin' shit like that, but you never do it.

GIRL: This time I will. I promise. I'm not foolin'. *(Waves knife at him)* I don't want to hurt you.

BOY: *(Grabs her wrist and then slips behind her. He takes the knife out of her hand and drops it on the floor)*

GIRL: *(Exhausted-she sags in his arms)* I'm so friggin' tired.

BOY: *(He moves away from her and picks up the knife and looks at it)* Me too. *(He drops the knife on the table)*

GIRL: I can't sleep. I can never get no sleep. *(Starts scratching or obsessively touching her face and looking out as if something horrible is there)* They won't let me sleep. They're always scratchin' and knockin' things over and they shit everywhere. They don't have no respect for their environment. See, if you don't sleep, your mind starts playin' tricks on you. You start seein' things.

BOY: *(Sits down on couch)* You're killin' me. You're drownin' and you won't let go. You're killin' me.

GIRL: *(Suddenly looks at him as if she is normal again)* Why do you have your coat on?

BOY: 'Cause I'm leavin'.

GIRL: *(Walks over to him and starts to pull off his coat)* Take it off. I don't like it when you wear your coat. I don't like it when you wear your coat inside the house. *(Starts checking his pockets)* Where's the money for the rent?

BOY: *(More to himself)* Money for the rent? Money for the fuckin' rent? Don't you listen to me? Don't you listen to a word I say? I'm talkin' and you just don't listen. I don't have no money. I didn't make no money. The money's gone, but it doesn't seem to go in your brain, in your head. Like how many times do I have to tell you that I got no money? I got nuthin'. How many times?

GIRL: *(Picking up the baby)* I think Baby needs new clothes.

BOY: Are you listenin' to me?

GIRL: *(Puts the baby back in the crib)* Me too. I think I need new clothes. Will you buy me some clothes?

BOY: *(Quietly)* Why? You never go anywhere.

GIRL: But I might if I had new clothes. If I had sumthin' to wear, sumthin' nice, then I might go out.

BOY: You won't go out. You never go out.

GIRL: *(Sits down beside him)* How come you don't got no money? I remember, you used to get money. Now all you got is holes in your arm. And you look like shit.

BOY: Holes in my arm? Yeah! That's where my money goes; up my arm, up my piggy bank. My money goes up my arm. I couldn't live, couldn't survive, if I didn't take that money and fill my arms, fill my arms with poison. *(Dreamily)* I just want to hide in my cloud, hide in my cloud and die.

GIRL: *(Looks at him as if he is very odd)* What happened to you? You used to ride a bike… Remember? *(Gets up quickly and looks through her photographs on the floor)* See, I found this picture. Do you remember? Do you remember this picture? *(Finds it)* See, you're ridin' a bike. How old were you?

BOY: *(Not paying attention)* What bike?

GIRL: *(Sits down beside him)* Look at the picture

BOY: *(Not looking)* What bike?

GIRL: *(Staring at him)* You got a bike.

BOY: *(Looks at her)* I don't remember no bike.

GIRL: Sure you do...Fire engine red. *(Thrusts photo in his face)* See...

BOY: *(Takes the picture)* Fire engine red. *(Getting excited)* Yeah, yeah. I had a bike. How could I forget? I remember the wind, like I was flyin', like I was breakin' the speed of sound, and the road, the road was where I was gonna go. I could be anythin' I wanted to be. Do anythin'. What happened to that bike? Do you remember what happened?

GIRL: *(Looking off into her own memories)* I remember that bike.

BOY: Ridin' like a captain of the air.

GIRL: I remember that bike.

BOY: Up through the air into the moon and the stars.

GIRL: *(Urging him on)* Yes.

BOY: Streamers on the handlebars.

GIRL: Yes!

BOY: I could go anywhere on that bike. *(Looks at picture as if something is unusual)* Look at that. I'm laughin'.

GIRL: That's why we should have a party.
Everybody has fun at a party. Everybody feels happy.
See the table. I set the table. What do you think?

BOY: *(Gets up)*...I gotta go.

GIRL: *(Subdued)* Why do you hate me?

BOY: I don't hate you. You're my blood.

GIRL: I'm your blood.

BOY: Yes, and my blood, it's poisoned.

GIRL: *(Gets up)* Why do you say stupid things like
that?

BOY: I say stupid things like that, because stupid
things like that are true.

GIRL: *(Trying to touch his face to find the answers)*
But I don't get what you mean? Are you trying to tell
me sumthin'? Is there sumthin' that you mean?

BOY: *(Turns away from her)* I don't mean nuthin'.

GIRL: You gotta mean sumthin'.

BOY: No...

GIRL: You gotta mean sumthin'. Everythin' means sumthin'.

BOY: No. Nuthin' means nuthin'.

GIRL:You don't make no sense.

BOY: *(Drops down on the mattress-Curls up in a ball)* You wouldn't understand.

GIRL: *(Kneels down beside him)* I wouldn't understand? No, no. I don't understand. I don't understand nuthin'. I don't get why you're so cold to me. Why you don't care. I try to be nice. I try to make things better. When the social assistance comes, I pay the rent, buy the food. I take care of us. But you, you just go out. You don't help, you don't help me. You just lie around the house all day and then go out at night. You don't know. You don't realize how good you got it. At night, what happens? Where do you go?

BOY: *(Sits up)* You don't wanna know. In here, you're safe. Nobody can touch you. In here is the dream. And the dream plays the same show over and over again. Yesterday the show was the same. *(Looks at her)* You said the same things, I said the same things, and tomorrow will be just like today. Only nobody's buyin' tickets to see this show. *(Out to audience)* Come one, come all, come and see the dream show. But nobody will come. Nope. Nobody will come. They won't come 'cause a what's outside, the thing outside. You see; out there, out in the world, there's nuthin', nuthin' but dark...Blind eyes and blank faces. Sure, they talk to you. They touch you…but they died a long time ago. Their bodies are cold. When I'm out there, I turn to nuthin'. I go invisible. Nobody can see me, but I can see them, I can see right through them, but I'm not there. So it's all right, it's okay. I'm floatin' on my cloud. My body has died, turned to dust and I'm floating, floatin' on my cloud. *(Turns to her)* Do you know what I mean?

GIRL: *(Afraid)* No, you're confusin' me. Where do you go?

BOY: *(Looks up)* Me? Nowhere. I don't go nowhere. There is nowhere. Just brick and stone. I hide in the goddamn brick and stone, I hide in the dark, in the shadows, in the cold sweat of the moon.

GIRL: *(Trying to cover his mouth)* Please stop talkin' like that! You're confusin' me! I don't know what you mean.

BOY: *(Grabs her hand away from his mouth)* I mean I hide. Out there I hide, disappear, melt away, turn into nuthin'. Nuthin' but a shadow in the dark.

GIRL: *(Backing up)* Please, please, please stop talkin' like that! Talk to me so that I can understand, so that I can understand what you're sayin'. You scare me when you talk like that.

BOY: *(Following her)* I haunt the streets like a blood suckin' vampire. I take my blood out and fill my veins with poison. *(He stops moving)*

GIRL: I'm scared for you. What happens out there? What happens?

BOY: *(Turns away)* Nuthin'...

GIRL: *(Getting increasingly agitated)* Nuthin'? Nuthin' happens? I don't believe you. Sumthin' happens. You don't do nuthin'. No one can do nuthin'. You're out for hours. You can't do nuthin' for hours. Its hard to do nuthin', to be nuthin', to think nuthin', to feel nuthin'. Tell me what you do.

BOY: *(Harshly)* I told you. I hide in the shadows and fill my arms with poison, killin' myself with poison and I don't care. Know what I mean? I kill myself and welcome it. I welcome the last breaths, the darkness

25

comin down, that black end of the road sleep. I welcome disappearin' in the dark, of never findin' my way home again.

GIRL: *(Unhappily)* I wish you wouldn't talk like that.

BOY: *(Snaps back to normal whatever normal is)* But I do, I do talk like that. That's how I talk. Why can't I talk like I talk?

GIRL: *(Looks for refuge in the images of her birthday party)* No. I want to talk about sumthin' nice. I want to go back to my eighth birthday party, *(Stares at one of the pictures on the floor, a photo of herself as a little girl)* See. Wasn't I pretty? See the ribbons. I want to go back

BOY: Nobody goes back.

GIRL: *(Remembering)* I just remember bein' in this room. I remember blowin' out the candles for the last time, and I remember the dark. I don't like the dark, 'cause in the dark, *(Afraid)* that's when you hear things. I hear them scurryin' about. They scurry, right? They scurry in the dark with their red eyes, watchin' me, always watchin' me, lookin' at me, and I can't see them, but they can see me. They look right through me, and I think about bein' alone here, with

26

nobody. No friends, no family. *(Angry)* And I get jealous. I get these feelin's. *(Drifting off)* Sometimes it seems to me that you'll never come back. And I wonder, I wonder; did I say sumthin' to scare you off? Did I do sumthin'? *(To him)* But then you come back. You always come back. And you got money. You always got money. Where do you get the money?

BOY: *(Tired of explaining)* I don't have no money

GIRL: No, you don't. You don't have money no more but you used to. *(In her head she sees a long-lost romantic evening)* Remember? You'd bring home take-out and we'd play music, and it was like we were out on a date and everythin' was special. Do you remember that?

BOY: *(Reliving a fond memory)* Yeah, I thought I was goin' places. That I had the world by the tail. People used to talk about my looks. What a good-lookin' boy I was.

GIRL: I thought the girl that married you would be so lucky. Remember the girls? I hated them. I was so jealous of them. I used to pray, I used to pray that the girls would go away, that they would leave us alone...*(Suddenly quiet)* And one day, they did.

BOY: And now there's nobody, nobody but us. *(Looks around at the mess in the apartment)* What do you do all day? In this goddamn apartment, what do you do all day?

GIRL: *(Evasive)* Things. I do things. I'm very busy. *(Emphatically)* I'm a very busy person.

BOY: *(Undeterred, he presses the attack)* What sorts of things? What sorts of things do you do? What do you do all day?

GIRL: *(Gets up suddenly)* Stop it! You're crazy! You need to see a psychiatrist. Yep. A psychiatrist. Fix your brain. Your head. Get some medication

BOY: *(Gets up and follows her)* What do you do all day?

GIRL: *(Trying to fight back)* Things, okay, I do things.

BOY: Really? What sort of things? What sorts of things do you do?

GIRL: *(Pacing)* Well, I do a lot of thinkin', I think all the time. I can't turn it off. I think and I think. And they just won't shut up. I try to shut them up, but they keep talkin, and talkin' and talkin'.

BOY: Yeah…Well, what do they say? What do these voices say? What do they talk about?

GIRL: *(Desperate, she suddenly stops)* Shh, they're listenin'. I need to get some sleep. *(Smiles weakly)* I'm afraid I'm losin' my mind. (*Trying to retreat into her happy memories*) I try to think of happy things. I try to think of sunshine and blue sky. Do you remember when we were little? Do you remember my birthday party? Do you remember if we had vanilla icin' with flowers, candy flowers that you saved for the end? Do you remember? Am I losin' my mind or is that true? Did that happen? *(The memory starts to fade away)*

BOY: *(Grabs his bag)* Shut up about that stupid party! I'm goin'!

GIRL: *(Pleading)* No. Don't go. I don't wanna be alone.

BOY: I can't stay.

GIRL: I'm always so alone. So scared.

BOY: *(Starts to go)* I can't handle this.

GIRL: What?

BOY: This bullshit. I can't handle it. I have to go. *(He starts to go again)*

GIRL: There's no bullshit here. *(She grabs him)* Wait!

BOY: What?

GIRL: *(Feigned cheerfulness)* There's sumthin' I want to ask you. Sumthin' I've been meanin' to ask you. Sumthin' that's been on my mind and-

BOY: What's that? What's been on your mind?

GIRL:I think a lot of things, ya know? I have nuthin' to do here but think. Thinkin' all sorts of things, crazy, crazy things. I had an idea about how to, I dunno, I gotta ask you sumthin'

BOY: What do you want to ask me?

GIRL: *(Doesn't respond)*

BOY: What do you want to ask me?

GIRL: *(Gives up)* I don't remember.

BOY: *(Starts to leave)* I'm goin'.

GIRL: *(Gets in his way)* Why don't you ever bring your friends home?

30

BOY: *(Insistent)* I have to go.

GIRL: Why don't you bring your friends here?

BOY: You think I have friends?

GIRL: You're out. Out there in the world. You must have friends, Girlfriends, friends of some kind.

BOY: *(Whining)* Please let me go.

GIRL: *(Weirdly flirtatious)* Are you shamed of me?

BOY: I don't have friends. I don't have nuthin'.

GIRL: *(Smiles)* You have me.

BOY: I have you. I don't want you, but, yeah, I have you.

GIRL: *(Suddenly brightening)* Yeah, you and me, we're like a fairy tale.

BOY: Some fairy tale.

GIRL: Yeah...This is our castle and you're my prince; my handsome prince.

BOY: *(Cynically)* Prince? No, I'm no prince, but maybe I can get you one. Drag one off the street. Just for you. You can usually find one huddled under an old blanket sharin' a bottle of sumthin'. A prince of princes!

GIRL: *(Ignoring him)* Yeah, because, sometimes when you're gone, like when you walk out that door, I don't think you're ever comin' back. *(Seeing an unhappy end for herself)* Sometimes when you're gone, I think I'm gonna be alone for ever, that I'll die here, like some crazy person. *(To him)* Am I crazy?

BOY: *(Evasively)* I dunno.

GIRL: *(Goes to the crib and gently picks up the baby)* Sometimes I think so, sometimes I think I'll do sumthin', sumthin' real bad. And like my baby, I wish it was real, like flesh and blood real, and then it could love me back, just like the way that I love her. With guck inside and organs and feelings, *(Stops suddenly)* no, no feelin's. We shouldn't have no feelin's. Feelin's are bad. *(Increasingly angry and cruel)* And if the baby was alive, then I could kill it. I could take out its eye and it would feel it and scream. And I could watch it hurt, *(Throws the baby on the floor)* instead of bangin' the goddamn thing on the floor and knowin' that it don't feel nuthin'! I could hurt it, *(Kneels down to pick up the baby and speaking with a softer tone of voice)* I could hurt the baby and then nobody could hurt me...Do you wanna know what I'm afraid of? Do you? Ask me what I'm afraid of? Go on; ask me?

BOY: *(Resignedly)* All right…What are you afraid of?

GIRL: You! I'm afraid of you.

BOY:Me? Why should you be afraid of me? I'm not nuthin'. Why should you be so afraid of me?

GIRL: *(Staring off)* I'm afraid you're gonna leave, gonna go away with your friends that I never see, go away and never come back, and then I'm gonna sit here, get stuck here, be trapped here, and when the sun goes down in the dark, when they come out at night and-

BOY: Well, why don't you go outside? Why don't you ever go outside?

GIRL: *(Sits on couch unhappily)* I told you I can't!

BOY: But there are people outside.

GIRL: *(Touching her hair)* I can't. I'm not pretty. No one would want me

BOY: *(Encouraging her, while sitting down beside her)* Sure they would. Like I told you before, you're a

very pretty girl. The boys will fall in love with you. *(Cynical)* Boys will pay for love.

GIRL: *(Acknowledging the depth of her madness)* You don't love me. You're a boy. You can't wait to leave. You been leavin' for a long time now. I'm not stupid. I might be strange. Weird. But I'm not stupid. I see things. Inside I'm ugly. My feelin's are all ugly. The only beautiful feelin's I have are for you, and they're all wrong, all messed up, all bad. And I know you'll leave me, and I'll do sumthin', sumthin' really bad. I'm gonna to do sumthin' real bad and you won't be able to stop me. You'll be gone. You'll be gone and take the sunshine with you and I will be left in the dark with my doll. That's what I think. Alone in the dark with my doll.

BOY: *(Changing the subject)* You should give that thing; that doll, a proper name.

GIRL: *(Suspiciously)* Why?

BOY: Things need names. People need names.

GIRL: *(Holds the baby out to him as if it is only a doll)* It's not a people. It's a cold hard bit of plastic. It needs no name.

BOY: *(Continuing)* Everythin' needs a name. Trees flowers, birds, they all need names.

GIRL: You don't have a name. I don't have a name. We don't have names. You're just the boy, and I'm just the girl. *(Suddenly stands up)* Give me a hug. Come on. Don't be a jerk. Give me a hug. *(The boy gets up)* One little hug can't hurt. *(They hug)* See, isn't that nice? You smell like outside. Trees n' flowers, cars n' fresh air.

BOY: You smell like shit. *(He sits back down)*

GIRL: Don't tease me. *(Kneels down at his feet)* When you're away, I think of you all the time. You're the only other person I know, so I think about you. Nobody else. All the time. I wish I could take you and eat you up piece by piece until there's nuthin' left, *(Starts to take off his shoes)* nuthin' left but your shoes because I wouldn't want to eat your shoes because they would be covered in dog shit. But I would eat everythin' up, but your shoes and you would be inside me and never be able to leave. I try. I try to hold on. Sometimes, I feel okay. Sometimes I see what I'm supposed to see. Say what I'm supposed to say. *(Places shoes under the couch)* Sometimes I feel what I'm supposed to feel, and sometimes I feel crazy. *(Getting excited as she climbs up on the couch beside him)* Real crazy. Losin' my life crazy. Sometimes I feel like I can't breathe. Sometimes I feel like doing sumthin', sumthin' wild! Do you ever feel that? Do you ever feel like doin' sumthin' wild?

BOY: Sometimes…Sometimes I feel like doin' sumthin'.

GIRL: Like what? Like what do you feel like doin'?

BOY: I dunno.. Sumthin'.

GIRL: I want us to be a family again.

BOY: Family?

GIRL: Don't you remember?

BOY: *(Darkly)* Yeah, I remember. The family from hell.

GIRL: Why did you say that? Just now. Family from hell. Why did you say that?

BOY: I remember why I turned out the way I did.

GIRL: Turned out?

BOY: Yup. Turned out.

GIRL: How did you turn out?

BOY: Like this.

GIRL: *(Desperate to understand his meaning and perhaps the answer to the puzzle)* How? You n' me? How did we turn out?

BOY: I would say more than a little messed up.

GIRL: *(She knows something traumatic has happened but can't remember it)* But didn't sumthin' happen to us? Didn't sumthin' turn us out this way?

BOY: *(He probably knows what happened but chooses not to think of it)* I dunno. Maybe. I think its best not to, y'know, think about it, think about things like that. I try not to think. Shut everythin' out. That's what I do. Keep the monsters out. I only wanna get by. Exist. Each minute, each second, each breath; they're like mountains. Ya just gotta make it over the next hill

GIRL: *(Gets up and goes to where the pictures are scattered on the floor)* Did I show you this, what I found?

BOY: *(Not really paying attention)* The pictures? Yes.

GIRL: No, no, sumthin' else, sumthin' else I found. Its so easy not to remember, to forget things. *(She finds the report card among the pictures and picks it up)*

BOY: What is it?

GIRL: *(Approaches him)* My report card from grade three. Remember when I was in the school play?

BOY: No.

GIRL: Yes you do. I was Charlie. Read this.

BOY: *(Starting to get up)* I have to go.

GIRL: Read it. I read it to Baby. Baby was very impressed.

BOY: I'm sure she was.

GIRL: Read it!

BOY: *(Takes card from her)* Shows attentiveness to her lessons. *(Hands it back to her)*

GIRL: *(Slowly sounding out the word)* Atten...tive...ness. *(She smiles)* Read more.

BOY: *(Getting up and looking for his bag)* I don't have time for this.

GIRL: Read some more.

BOY: *(Takes the card)* Shows potential.

GIRL: Do you think I got potential?

BOY: I dunno. Maybe. Aren't we born with potential?

GIRL: Next! Read the next bit. Go on. Read it.

BOY: Writes very neatly.

GIRL: *(Happy)* See! I used to write good. *(Correcting herself)* Neatly. I wonder what happened. I could've been a secretary, like for a lawyer or a doctor or sumthin', 'cause I had potential. See Baby; I had potential.

BOY: (*Lost in his own thoughts*) I wanted to be a cowboy.

GIRL: Now, that's stupid.

BOY: *(Wishing he was a different kind of person in a different kind of world)* No, it's not. Cowboys are heroes. They don't let people bully them. They don't let anybody tell them what to do, plus they get to ride horses. They can even ride a horse into the wild blue yonder.

GIRL: We should go ridin' someday. Didn't we used to go ridin'?

BOY: How can you go ridin'? You won't even go outside that door.

GIRL: But if we went ridin' I might.

BOY: Don't be stupid.

GIRL:Don't call me stupid! I'm not stupid. I have potential. *(A new strange thought has penetrated her brain)* Remember our mother?

BOY: Yeah, Did you know that rats and humans share many of the same characteristics? They eat the same food, live in the same places, are very sociable and carry disease. *(The power suddenly goes out-Now there is a red light suggesting darkness-He looks up confused for a moment)* Shit. *(He goes to the light switch and tries it a couple of times)* I never had a mother. I was born in garbage, out of the rotting stink of night. My mother now is a needle. *(He suddenly looks at her and grabs at her dress)* What is this? Who do you think you are in that piece of shit dress?

GIRL: *(Hurt)* I did it for you. I thought you'd like it. I thought it would be nice.

BOY: *(Being deliberately mean as if he can't help himself)* I hate it. It's stupid. *(Starts to rifle through the dresser drawers looking for drugs)*

GIRL: I thought it would be nice to dress up on my birthday. I used to dress up on my birthday. I used to, but who cares? Who gives a shit? You? You don't care. You hardly say nuthin' to me, nuthin' at all.

BOY: *(Finds his drugs. During her next speech, he takes off his belt, ties it around his arm and proceeds to shoot up)*

GIRL: *(As he does his drugs she starts going crazy when she sees what he is doing)* What's he doin'? What's he doin'? What's he doin'? You can't trust food that you can't see being prepared. Someone might put foreign objects, like razor blades in your pizza, or they might piss on your precious Chinese food. Out there, out there, people are so angry that they can't control themselves and they strike out at you. They put poison in your food…*(Suddenly desperately calm)* Last night I had a dream, a strange, strange dream. Mother was in a little boat dressed all in white, and she had a white…parasol, those little umbrellas, like they had in the old days. And she was singin', singin' in her little boat. She didn't sing words, just these beautiful, beautiful notes.

Pretty Pieces

BOY: I don't want to talk about her.

GIRL: *(Drops to her knees on the mattress)* And you were all twisted on the banks of the stream in some ugly old tree. And your eyes…I could hear you cryin', like you were trapped and couldn't move, couldn't reach out …And me? Well, the water wasn't water, it was made of blood, and I was tryin' to reach you, tryin' to swim through the stream and my arms were gettin' so tired and I was being pulled under where I couldn't breathe and then I heard screamin' and I woke up,. Do you ever have dreams like that? Do you ever see stuff like that? When I woke up, I could hear voices, but they weren't talkin' to me. They were outside and I was just a doll in a box without feelin's, who watches life go by, but for one minute the doll wakes up and does sumthin', for one minute the doll comes to life and does sumthin', does sumthin' awful, because a doll; it don't know the difference between wrong and right. I'm so tired. Lie down with me for a bit and we can sleep and the dream will be over.. *(Reaches out to him)* Lie down with me. Lie down with me for a minute.

BOY: *(Feeling fuzzy because of the drugs)* But I gotta go. *(Slowly lifts up his foot and realizes he isn't wearing his shoes and vaguely looks around)*

GIRL: I know, but let's lie down together one last time.

BOY: *(Confused)* One last time?

GIRL: Yeah. Lie with me one last time and then everythin' will be all right. Everythin' will be better. Come here.

BOY: One last time?

GIRL: Before you go. One last time.

BOY: And no more games?

GIRL: One last time.

BOY: *(Sits down groggily on mattress)* I dunno. I gotta be somewhere. He's expectin' me. He's waitin' for me. *(Looking around the apartment as if seeing it for the first time-This next bit is spoken dreamily-not angrily)* Why don't you clean up? Why don't you clean up the *(Considers the word god damned fearfully as if God has abandoned them)* god...damned place? Why don't you ever make it look nice? You know, that's why...that's why I never bring anyone here. It's embarrassin'. It's a pig...sty. You could never expect me to bring anyone here...I mean, what could I say?

43

Pretty Pieces

GIRL: *(Looking through the pictures)*

BOY: *(Sees his shoes under the couch and points)* Shoes...

GIRL: Do you remember these ones? See, we're horseback ridin'. There's a picture of you, too. I'm on the white pony and you're on that blotchy one. *(Laughs)* You look so sad.

BOY: I remember. My horse wouldn't go.

GIRL: No. It wouldn't. You weren't good with animals. Not like me. .

BOY: You need to get a life.

GIRL: I have a life. I'm a girl trapped in a box, fed like a little wild animal by my brother and I have grown quite fond of him, of my brother, because he feeds me and keeps me goin'. And I think my feelin's are wrong, wrong, wrong, wrong, but I can't help them and that's why I wish you would bring home someone else, so that I could fall in love with them, because as you see, I'm afraid, and I want to have a real baby, so I can smash this baby's face in, sumthin' for me to love. Are you goin' to give me a baby?

BOY: Why do you say shit like that?

GIRL: Sumthin' happened a long time ago.

BOY: Sumthin' always happens a long time ago.

GIRL: I think sumthin' bad happened, but I can't tell. I can't tell what happened. There's not enough evidence. See these pictures, see; they're like pieces of the puzzle, but I can't figure them out. There's not enough of them. It's like the puzzle is so big and we only got a few pieces and it's not enough. Is it because I was attentive? Is that it? That I showed potential. That I wrote good. Are those the clues? Is it me on the pony? You on yours? Is it you on your bike? Is it me at my birthday party? Like, are these the only clues? Where did the baby come from? Whose baby is it? Is it mine? I dunno. And how long have we been here? We don't even have a friggin' clock in here. I never know what time it is. Why are we like this?

BOY: I dunno, I never look at things that deeply. I remember what I wanna remember. I remember the things that I like and the things that I don't like, I don't remember.

GIRL: What the hell is that sposed to mean?

BOY: It means what it means…*(Suddenly feeling bad for her)* I'm sorry.

GIRL: Sorry about what?

BOY: 'Bout the things I said, about forgettin' your birthday.

GIRL: *(Smiling)* You wouldn't be you if you didn't forget.

BOY: No, I wouldn't be me…I wouldn't be me.

GIRL: Just rest a little.

BOY: *(lies down)*

GIRL: Tell me about your friend, your new friend. What's he like? Is he nice?

BOY: He's older. He lives in a nice apartment. His wife just left him and he's very lonely. We met at a party. He's an artist, a painter. He's wise. I like that. He seems to understand. That first night, we got very drunk. I woke up in his bed. Turns out it was his apartment, the party, it was in his apartment. I had met some friends, well I don't have friends, people I knew and they were sayin' they were goin' to this party and this guy, he liked boys and he was havin' a party and there was drugs and food. I was hungry. I'm

46

always hungry and the party was fun, took me away from me for awhile and then like I said, I met him and I felt so warm and comfortable. And he liked me.

GIRL: Did you like him?

BOY: I don't know. Does it matter? But we can talk about things, about anythin'. And I've finally started facin' up to, I dunno, what's happened, findin' out some things, things about myself and he's a successful artist. He has money. And he likes me.

GIRL: *(Hopefully)* Did you tell him about me? Maybe I could live there, too. If he has enough money.

BOY: Well, I told him about you, but he thinks, he says, he don't know if we're good for each other. He thinks I should get away from you, for a while, for a bit, 'cause we bring each other down. We're like trapped in this cage and he thinks I would be better off without you, and you would be better off without me, you know, stand on your own two feet. Just like me, I gotta learn to stand on my own two feet.

GIRL So you're gonna leave me?

BOY: Don't you see? It will be better for both of us. We're not doin' each other no good. Not like this.

47

GIRL: Hmm. I thought in the whole wide world that we were special, that we were the only two people like us in the world, that we were sposed to be together forever, 'cause we shared sumthin', 'cause when we were younger, sumthin' happened and somehow if we stayed together, it would come out all right, somehow, it would turn out good, but you're makin' it all wrong. You can't leave me. I can't let you leave me. Everythin' would go all wrong. If you leave, there would be no more us. That can't happen. How could there be no more us? I wish that there was some sorta answer. I wish I knew what happened, back when I was eight. I wish I knew the answer to the mystery, but I don't. I don't know nuthin'. All I know is that sumthin' happened, sumthin' happened to us. I wish there were more clues. I wish I understood, but it's just a jigsaw puzzle without enough pieces. I'm the girl and you're the boy and we 're the only two people in this world. Broken dolls in a box. And I was hopin' for some cake and some vanilla icin' with candles, like angels in the dark, and my name in candy letters, save them to the end, Eat them at the end. But I don't think I'm ever gonna get that cake and I don't think I'm ever gonna unnerstan' nuthin'. Go to sleep. *(Puts pillow over his face)* Go to sleep.

BOY: *(Starts to struggle)*

GIRL: No, No. Don't fight me. Don't fight me. Don't fight me. Don't fight me.

BOY: *(He fights for a moment and then goes limp)*

GIRL: *(Lifts up the pillow and examines his face)* Look Baby; he's asleep, *(Starts to caress his face and kisses his lips)* Isn't he beautiful? And now he'll never go away. He'll never leave us. *(She places the baby beside the Boy)* Stay there Baby. I'll be back. *(Gets up and goes to the kitchen table and picks up the sharp knife and stares at it)* When I was eight years old, I had sumthin', I had potential. *(Walks back to where the Boy is lying on the mattress)* I coulda been anythin', anythin' I wanted to be. *(Drops down on the mattress upstage of the boy)* I coulda been a secretary, I coulda been normal, but then sumthin' happened to me. I don't know what, but I guess sumthin' always happens. I acted in a play once, a school play, a long time ago. I played Charlie. *(Slowly she plays with the knife)* I don't remember what happened at the end. I don't remember what I did at the end, but when the play was over the lights went out. The lights went out and everybody went home. And when I was eight years old, I blew out the candles for the very last time. I was happy for the very last time. My brother

49

and me; we used to be normal. We rode horses and bikes. We dreamed of being cowboys and princesses. We acted in school plays...but then sumthin' happened. Sumthin' bad happened. Sumthin' really bad. *(She raises the knife above her head with both hands. She is about to plunge it into her stomach when there is a quick blackout)*

FINI

ABOUT THE AUTHOR

Charles Robertson is a playwright and director in Canada who has been involved in all facets of theatre. He has written a number of plays for young people, including *Ghost of the Tree* and *Til the Boys Come Home.* With partner Anne Marie Mortensen, he runs Bottle Tree Productions at www.bottletreeinc.com

Bottle Tree Productions offers free acting advice and monologues for aspiring actors.

Bottle Tree Productions One Act Play Competition for Writers has a One Thousand Dollar First Prize and closes on November 30th of each year.

CPSIA information can be obtained
at www.ICGtesting.com
Printed in the USA
LVOW04s2152290116
472894LV00025B/661/P